# BE THE LEAD

## A PLANNER TO BECOME THE HERO IN YOUR DAILY LIFE STORY

*Written & Produced by*

**SARA QUIRICONI**

You Are The Creator — the Writer, Producer, Director and Actor of your own story. BE THE LEAD, be the Hero and Create Consciously.

BETHELEAD.CLUB

# BREAKDOWN

## SYNOPSIS OF THIS PLANNER

### WELCOME NOTE

*Lights, camera, action!* Just as an actor brings a script to life on stage or screen, a planner plays a crucial role in bringing your life story to fruition. Think of your planner as the guiding script that helps you navigate through each day with purpose and intention.

As an actress myself, being an actor is not just a profession, but a way of life. It requires a unique mindset and an unwavering passion for the craft requiring dedication, direction and consistency daily.

Just like an actor studies their lines and understands the motivations of their character, a planner helps you establish healthy habits and routines that align with your goals. It provides structure and direction, allowing you to make the most of each moment or beat in your days.

Your planner is not just a tool for jotting down appointments and deadlines; it's a powerful instrument for shaping your destiny. It empowers you to take control of your narrative and create the life you envision.

Much like how actors rehearse daily to perfect their craft, using a planner enables you to practice positive habits consistently. By mapping out your days in advance, you can prioritize tasks, allocate time for self-care, and ensure progress towards your daily and overall objectives.

Remember that every great story has its ups and downs, or climaxes and catharsis. Your planner serves as the compass that guides you through both triumphs and challenges. It helps you stay focused on what truly matters amidst the chaos of everyday life.

So grab hold of your metaphorical script – your planner – and step into the role of the protagonist in your own life story. Embrace each day as an opportunity for growth, learning, and fulfillment. With dedication and commitment to using your planner effectively, watch as your life unfolds into an extraordinary masterpiece worth celebrating. Life is a game we play, awaiting you to be the hero. Expand, take charge and take risks, becoming the lead.

*Sarl*

**While you can't change the beginning, you can start in the NOW and create the middle and craft the ending of your life story.**

— *SARA QUIRICONI*

## HOW TO USE THIS PLANNER

If you've ever been on a professional movie or production set, you've probably come across a piece of paper known as a call sheet. A call sheet is more than just scheduling, but as a tool to keep an entire production on the same wavelength.

As a very organized and creative creature (or recovering perfectionist, some may call it), since I can remember I've been a dedicated end user and doodler of calendars , journals and planners. From my days on set, I realized how similar a call sheet was to a daily planner. How the character development and systems I've learned and used were similar to goal setting and personal growth. Further, how if you really want to be the lead in a film or similar role, you need to show up consistently, allowing the character to evolve with strategy, flexibility and dedication.

The development for BE THE LEAD Planner occured when I was seeking a planner for myself that would encapsulate all that I needed on one sheet for a day at a time, that I could easily plan out and answer to strategize on my journey. It would ask poignant questions that would prompt beats of emotional change and actionable cues to give myself space to grow and to be challenged.

While there are many planners out there, there wasn't one that exactly hit the mark for me. So, I made my own, and decided to overlap my craft of acting and the development of my daily habits and lifesyle.

Hence, the creation of BE THE LEAD Planner.

## THE DAILY SELF CALL SHEET

Each daily self call sheet has two columns, with 95% of the writing done in the morning to set you up for your day ahead. After all, the best spent time in a production actually lies in the pre-production phase, ensuring the days ahead would be strategized, carefully coordinated and flow with greatest ease. Time is money, people!

In the planner, the bottom left is reserved for a daily reflection. This isn't to get lazy at the end of your day, but rather to set you up for success for the following day. Taking knowledge you've learned from that day from your life set, you can compound those tools to better formulate the day ahead filling out the following day's call sheet.

The questions are designed to get you clear and focused on your day ahead, having a powerful inner monologue to fuel your passion and purpose and be able to handle any obstacle ahead. With clear goals ahead, knowing a director (or script supervisor) could give you slight reminders and cues at any moment, just in case you missed a line, you will know how to feel empowered by your day to be able to call it a successful wrap at the end. I can promise you, the producer sleeps much more peacefully knowing the set was a success, on time and within budget.

## END OF WEEK WRAP UP

There's seven days for each week set, with a reset at the end called the Director's Cut to reflect back on your lead character's development. The goal here is to see what worked, what can add to the following week and what can keep you on your directed path to lead in your life in your week to week progress.

I encourage you to outline your days as much as you can possible using either 30-minute or hourly increments to time block your creative endeavors. Write out items such as meditation and exercise daily as part of your structure, tracking any intentions or character notes that arise.

Above all, remember this is play and to have fun in the process. The jouney becomes that much more enjoyable – most likely, successful – in doing so. Ready on set? Let's begin!

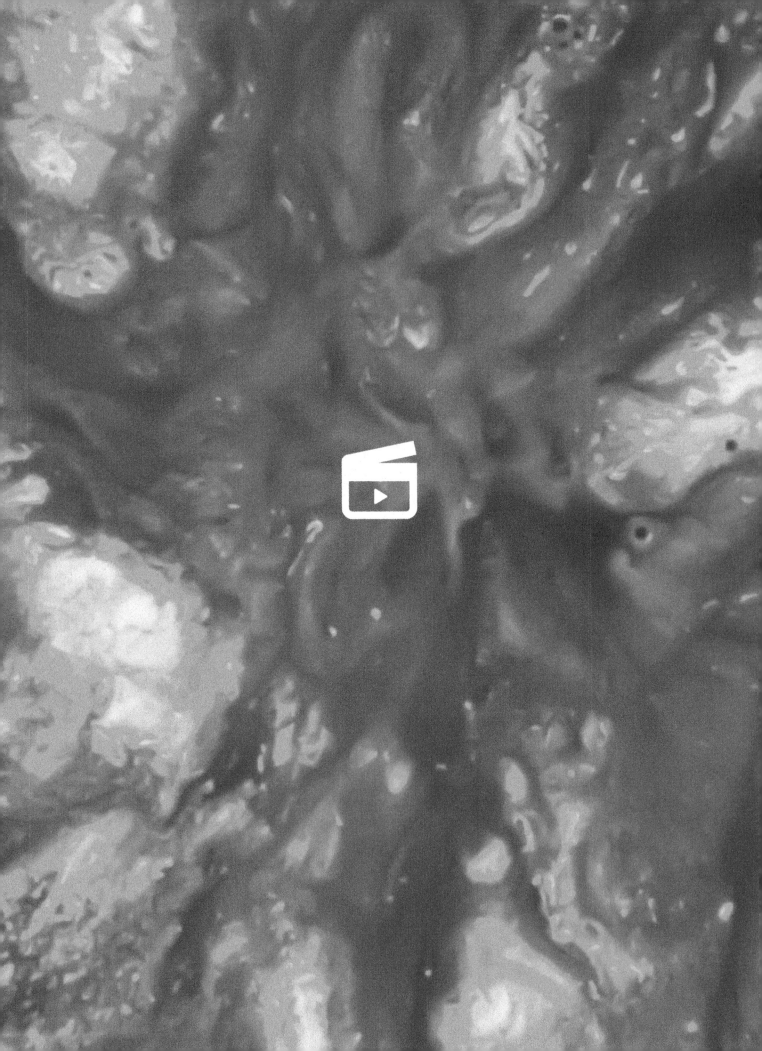

Create. Take risks. Live your passion. Pursue purpose. Fail forward. Live free. Be your own hero. Be the lead.

— *SARA QUIRICONI*

# CREATING YOUR CHARACTER

Take a moment to breathe, reflect, and visualize your leading character. After oberserving your hero mentally, take the time to answer the following. Remember, your character is on a development arc, not a perfected end goal. Progress, not perfection, is key. Have fun!

## ROUTINE & HABITS

What is your lead character's daily routine like? Morning and evening routines? Get as detailed as possible here.

_____
_____
_____
_____

## COMMUNICATION & CONFLICT

How does your lead character handle an antagonist conversation? What's one thing s/he needs to communicate? How does that feel?

_____
_____
_____
_____

## PROFESSIONAL DEVELOPMENT

What is your lead character's career goals, long-term and short-term? Write out the feeling of achieving one, or more, of those.

_____
_____
_____
_____

## HEALTH & WELL-BEING

What does your lead character do on a daily basis for fitness, nutrition, mental health, connect with others, and to spiritually ground?

_____
_____
_____
_____

## PLEASURE & LEISURE

What's something FUN your lead character likes to do in his/her free time? How will you schedule in time for this daily/weekly?

_____
_____
_____

## CORE VALUES & NEEDS

What are the core values of your lead character? What are his/her needs in this moment to match those core values?

_____
_____
_____
_____

# OVERALL OBJECTIVE

Each moment leads up to a greater whole. Looking at the weeks ahead, what goals can you set that will add to the overall objective of your purpose, passion and personal WHY for you lead character? This will shift, grow and build over time with momentum.

## OBJECTIVE WORD

Leading from your heart, what's the most meaningful achievement for you in life?

_____
_____
_____
_____

## EMOTIONAL COMPONENT

How will it feel having achieved this objective? Be descriptive: use color, emotion, visuals, bodily experiences, whatever arises for you.

_____
_____
_____
_____

## ACTION TOOLS

What tools will you need, or employ, to achieve this objective? Director's note: consistency creates successes.

_____
_____
_____
_____

## THE OSCAR MOMENT

How can you define having achieved that objective or goal? What are the markers of success, or your definition of is?

_____
_____
_____
_____

# DAILY SELF CALL SHEET

DATE

M  T  W  T  F  S  S

## TOP THREE PRIORITIES

1.

2.

3.

## TODAY'S INNER MONOLOGUE MESSAGE

## TODAY'S HIGHLIGHT AHEAD

## TODAY'S ONE WORD OBJECTIVE

## POTENTIAL OBSTACLE

## HOW I CAN PREPARE FOR THIS

## A DIRECTOR WOULD REMIND ME

## I COULD CALL TODAY A SUCCESSFUL WRAP WHEN

## TODAY I AM GRATEFUL FOR

## REFLECT AND CELEBRATE (EVENING)

## SCHEDULE

05:00 - MORNING ROUTINE

06:00

07:00

08:00

09:00

10:00

11:00

12:00

13:00

14:00

15:00

16:00

17:00

18:00

19:00

20:00 - EVENING ROUTINE

# DAILY SELF CALL SHEET

DATE

M  T  W  T  F  S  S

## TOP THREE PRIORITIES

1.

2.

3.

## TODAY'S INNER MONOLOGUE MESSAGE

## TODAY'S HIGHLIGHT AHEAD

## TODAY'S ONE WORD OBJECTIVE

## POTENTIAL OBSTACLE

## HOW I CAN PREPARE FOR THIS

## A DIRECTOR WOULD REMIND ME

## I COULD CALL TODAY A SUCCESSFUL WRAP WHEN

## TODAY I AM GRATEFUL FOR

## REFLECT AND CELEBRATE (EVENING)

## SCHEDULE

05:00 - MORNING ROUTINE

06:00

07:00

08:00

09:00

10:00

11:00

12:00

13:00

14:00

15:00

16:00

17:00

18:00

19:00

20:00 - EVENING ROUTINE

# DAILY SELF CALL SHEET

DATE

M   T   W   T   F   S   S

## TOP THREE PRIORITIES

1.

2.

3.

## TODAY'S INNER MONOLOGUE MESSAGE

## TODAY'S HIGHLIGHT AHEAD

## TODAY'S ONE WORD OBJECTIVE

## POTENTIAL OBSTACLE

## HOW I CAN PREPARE FOR THIS

## A DIRECTOR WOULD REMIND ME

## I COULD CALL TODAY A SUCCESSFUL WRAP WHEN

## TODAY I AM GRATEFUL FOR

## REFLECT AND CELEBRATE (EVENING)

## SCHEDULE

05:00 - MORNING ROUTINE

06:00

07:00

08:00

09:00

10:00

11:00

12:00

13:00

14:00

15:00

16:00

17:00

18:00

19:00

20:00 - EVENING ROUTINE

# DAILY SELF CALL SHEET

**TOP THREE PRIORITIES**

1.

2.

3.

**TODAY'S INNER MONOLOGUE MESSAGE**

**TODAY'S HIGHLIGHT AHEAD**

**TODAY'S ONE WORD OBJECTIVE**

**POTENTIAL OBSTACLE**

**HOW I CAN PREPARE FOR THIS**

**A DIRECTOR WOULD REMIND ME**

**I COULD CALL TODAY A SUCCESSFUL WRAP WHEN**

**TODAY I AM GRATEFUL FOR**

**REFLECT AND CELEBRATE (EVENING)**

**SCHEDULE**

05:00 - MORNING ROUTINE

06:00

07:00

08:00

09:00

10:00

11:00

12:00

13:00

14:00

15:00

16:00

17:00

18:00

19:00

20:00 - EVENING ROUTINE

# DAILY SELF CALL SHEET

DATE _____

M  T  W  T  F  S  S

## TOP THREE PRIORITIES

1. _____

2. _____

3. _____

## TODAY'S INNER MONOLOGUE MESSAGE

## TODAY'S HIGHLIGHT AHEAD

## TODAY'S ONE WORD OBJECTIVE

## POTENTIAL OBSTACLE

## HOW I CAN PREPARE FOR THIS

## A DIRECTOR WOULD REMIND ME

## I COULD CALL TODAY A SUCCESSFUL WRAP WHEN

## TODAY I AM GRATEFUL FOR

## REFLECT AND CELEBRATE (EVENING)

## SCHEDULE

05:00 - MORNING ROUTINE

06:00

07:00

08:00

09:00

10:00

11:00

12:00

13:00

14:00

15:00

16:00

17:00

18:00

19:00

20:00 - EVENING ROUTINE

# DAILY SELF CALL SHEET

DATE

M  T  W  T  F  S  S

## TOP THREE PRIORITIES

1.

2.

3.

## TODAY'S INNER MONOLOGUE MESSAGE

## TODAY'S HIGHLIGHT AHEAD

## TODAY'S ONE WORD OBJECTIVE

## POTENTIAL OBSTACLE

## HOW I CAN PREPARE FOR THIS

## A DIRECTOR WOULD REMIND ME

## I COULD CALL TODAY A SUCCESSFUL WRAP WHEN

## TODAY I AM GRATEFUL FOR

## REFLECT AND CELEBRATE (EVENING)

## SCHEDULE

05:00 - MORNING ROUTINE

06:00

07:00

08:00

09:00

10:00

11:00

12:00

13:00

14:00

15:00

16:00

17:00

18:00

19:00

20:00 - EVENING ROUTINE

# DAILY SELF CALL SHEET

DATE

M  T  W  T  F  S  S

## TOP THREE PRIORITIES

1.

2.

3.

## TODAY'S INNER MONOLOGUE MESSAGE

## TODAY'S HIGHLIGHT AHEAD

## TODAY'S ONE WORD OBJECTIVE

## POTENTIAL OBSTACLE

## HOW I CAN PREPARE FOR THIS

## A DIRECTOR WOULD REMIND ME

## I COULD CALL TODAY A SUCCESSFUL WRAP WHEN

## TODAY I AM GRATEFUL FOR

## REFLECT AND CELEBRATE (EVENING)

## SCHEDULE

05:00 - MORNING ROUTINE

06:00

07:00

08:00

09:00

10:00

11:00

12:00

13:00

14:00

15:00

16:00

17:00

18:00

19:00

20:00 - EVENING ROUTINE

# DIRECTOR'S CUT

### TOP THREE WINS THIS WEEK

1.

2.

3.

### WHAT DID I LEARN THIS WEEK

### WHAT CAN I LET GO OF

### WHAT WORKED WELL THIS WEEK

### WHAT CAN I LOOK FORWARD TO

### IS THERE ANYTHING I'M AVOIDING

### HOW CAN I ACCOMPLISH THIS NEXT WEEK

### WHAT'S MY BIGGEST PRIORITY THIS WEEK AHEAD

### ADDITIONAL NOTES

# DAILY SELF CALL SHEET

**TOP THREE PRIORITIES**

1.

2.

3.

**TODAY'S INNER MONOLOGUE MESSAGE**

**TODAY'S HIGHLIGHT AHEAD**

**TODAY'S ONE WORD OBJECTIVE**

**POTENTIAL OBSTACLE**

**HOW I CAN PREPARE FOR THIS**

**A DIRECTOR WOULD REMIND ME**

**I COULD CALL TODAY A SUCCESSFUL WRAP WHEN**

**TODAY I AM GRATEFUL FOR**

**REFLECT AND CELEBRATE (EVENING)**

**SCHEDULE**

05:00 - MORNING ROUTINE

06:00

07:00

08:00

09:00

10:00

11:00

12:00

13:00

14:00

15:00

16:00

17:00

18:00

19:00

20:00 - EVENING ROUTINE

# DAILY SELF CALL SHEET

DATE _____

M  T  W  T  F  S  S

## TOP THREE PRIORITIES

1. _____

2. _____

3. _____

## TODAY'S INNER MONOLOGUE MESSAGE

## TODAY'S HIGHLIGHT AHEAD

## TODAY'S ONE WORD OBJECTIVE

## POTENTIAL OBSTACLE

## HOW I CAN PREPARE FOR THIS

## A DIRECTOR WOULD REMIND ME

## I COULD CALL TODAY A SUCCESSFUL WRAP WHEN

## TODAY I AM GRATEFUL FOR

## REFLECT AND CELEBRATE (EVENING)

## SCHEDULE

05:00 - MORNING ROUTINE

06:00

07:00

08:00

09:00

10:00

11:00

12:00

13:00

14:00

15:00

16:00

17:00

18:00

19:00

20:00 - EVENING ROUTINE

# DAILY SELF CALL SHEET

## TOP THREE PRIORITIES

1.

2.

3.

## TODAY'S INNER MONOLOGUE MESSAGE

## TODAY'S HIGHLIGHT AHEAD

## TODAY'S ONE WORD OBJECTIVE

## POTENTIAL OBSTACLE

## HOW I CAN PREPARE FOR THIS

## A DIRECTOR WOULD REMIND ME

## I COULD CALL TODAY A SUCCESSFUL WRAP WHEN

## TODAY I AM GRATEFUL FOR

## REFLECT AND CELEBRATE (EVENING)

## SCHEDULE

05:00 - MORNING ROUTINE

06:00

07:00

08:00

09:00

10:00

11:00

12:00

13:00

14:00

15:00

16:00

17:00

18:00

19:00

20:00 - EVENING ROUTINE

# DAILY SELF CALL SHEET

DATE

M  T  W  T  F  S  S

## TOP THREE PRIORITIES

1.

2.

3.

## TODAY'S INNER MONOLOGUE MESSAGE

## TODAY'S HIGHLIGHT AHEAD

## TODAY'S ONE WORD OBJECTIVE

## POTENTIAL OBSTACLE

## HOW I CAN PREPARE FOR THIS

## A DIRECTOR WOULD REMIND ME

## I COULD CALL TODAY A SUCCESSFUL WRAP WHEN

## TODAY I AM GRATEFUL FOR

## REFLECT AND CELEBRATE (EVENING)

## SCHEDULE

05:00 - MORNING ROUTINE

06:00

07:00

08:00

09:00

10:00

11:00

12:00

13:00

14:00

15:00

16:00

17:00

18:00

19:00

20:00 - EVENING ROUTINE

# DAILY SELF CALL SHEET

DATE _____

M  T  W  T  F  S  S

## TOP THREE PRIORITIES

1. _____

2. _____

3. _____

## TODAY'S INNER MONOLOGUE MESSAGE

## TODAY'S HIGHLIGHT AHEAD

## TODAY'S ONE WORD OBJECTIVE

## POTENTIAL OBSTACLE

## HOW I CAN PREPARE FOR THIS

## A DIRECTOR WOULD REMIND ME

## I COULD CALL TODAY A SUCCESSFUL WRAP WHEN

## TODAY I AM GRATEFUL FOR

## REFLECT AND CELEBRATE (EVENING)

## SCHEDULE

05:00 - MORNING ROUTINE

06:00

07:00

08:00

09:00

10:00

11:00

12:00

13:00

14:00

15:00

16:00

17:00

18:00

19:00

20:00 - EVENING ROUTINE

# DAILY SELF CALL SHEET

DATE

M  T  W  T  F  S  S

## TOP THREE PRIORITIES

1.

2.

3.

## TODAY'S INNER MONOLOGUE MESSAGE

## TODAY'S HIGHLIGHT AHEAD

## TODAY'S ONE WORD OBJECTIVE

## POTENTIAL OBSTACLE

## HOW I CAN PREPARE FOR THIS

## A DIRECTOR WOULD REMIND ME

## I COULD CALL TODAY A SUCCESSFUL WRAP WHEN

## TODAY I AM GRATEFUL FOR

## REFLECT AND CELEBRATE (EVENING)

## SCHEDULE

05:00 - MORNING ROUTINE

06:00

07:00

08:00

09:00

10:00

11:00

12:00

13:00

14:00

15:00

16:00

17:00

18:00

19:00

20:00 - EVENING ROUTINE

# DAILY SELF CALL SHEET

DATE

M  T  W  T  F  S  S

## TOP THREE PRIORITIES

1.

2.

3.

## TODAY'S INNER MONOLOGUE MESSAGE

## TODAY'S HIGHLIGHT AHEAD

## TODAY'S ONE WORD OBJECTIVE

## POTENTIAL OBSTACLE

## HOW I CAN PREPARE FOR THIS

## A DIRECTOR WOULD REMIND ME

## I COULD CALL TODAY A SUCCESSFUL WRAP WHEN

## TODAY I AM GRATEFUL FOR

## REFLECT AND CELEBRATE (EVENING)

## SCHEDULE

05:00 - MORNING ROUTINE

06:00

07:00

08:00

09:00

10:00

11:00

12:00

13:00

14:00

15:00

16:00

17:00

18:00

19:00

20:00 - EVENING ROUTINE

# DIRECTOR'S CUT

**TOP THREE WINS THIS WEEK**

1.

2.

3.

**WHAT DID I LEARN THIS WEEK**

**WHAT CAN I LET GO OF**

**WHAT WORKED WELL THIS WEEK**

**WHAT CAN I LOOK FORWARD TO**

**IS THERE ANYTHING I'M AVOIDING**

**HOW CAN I ACCOMPLISH THIS NEXT WEEK**

**WHAT'S MY BIGGEST PRIORITY THIS WEEK AHEAD**

**ADDITIONAL NOTES**

# DAILY SELF CALL SHEET

DATE

M  T  W  T  F  S  S

## TOP THREE PRIORITIES

1.

2.

3.

## TODAY'S INNER MONOLOGUE MESSAGE

## TODAY'S HIGHLIGHT AHEAD

## TODAY'S ONE WORD OBJECTIVE

## POTENTIAL OBSTACLE

## HOW I CAN PREPARE FOR THIS

## A DIRECTOR WOULD REMIND ME

## I COULD CALL TODAY A SUCCESSFUL WRAP WHEN

## TODAY I AM GRATEFUL FOR

## REFLECT AND CELEBRATE (EVENING)

## SCHEDULE

05:00 - MORNING ROUTINE

06:00

07:00

08:00

09:00

10:00

11:00

12:00

13:00

14:00

15:00

16:00

17:00

18:00

19:00

20:00 - EVENING ROUTINE

# DAILY SELF CALL SHEET

DATE _____

M  T  W  T  F  S  S

## TOP THREE PRIORITIES

1. _____
2. _____
3. _____

## TODAY'S INNER MONOLOGUE MESSAGE

## TODAY'S HIGHLIGHT AHEAD

## TODAY'S ONE WORD OBJECTIVE

## POTENTIAL OBSTACLE

## HOW I CAN PREPARE FOR THIS

## A DIRECTOR WOULD REMIND ME

## I COULD CALL TODAY A SUCCESSFUL WRAP WHEN

## TODAY I AM GRATEFUL FOR

## REFLECT AND CELEBRATE (EVENING)

## SCHEDULE

05:00 - MORNING ROUTINE

06:00

07:00

08:00

09:00

10:00

11:00

12:00

13:00

14:00

15:00

16:00

17:00

18:00

19:00

20:00 - EVENING ROUTINE

# DAILY SELF CALL SHEET

DATE

M   T   W   T   F   S   S

## TOP THREE PRIORITIES

1.

2.

3.

## TODAY'S INNER MONOLOGUE MESSAGE

## TODAY'S HIGHLIGHT AHEAD

## TODAY'S ONE WORD OBJECTIVE

## POTENTIAL OBSTACLE

## HOW I CAN PREPARE FOR THIS

## A DIRECTOR WOULD REMIND ME

## I COULD CALL TODAY A SUCCESSFUL WRAP WHEN

## TODAY I AM GRATEFUL FOR

## REFLECT AND CELEBRATE (EVENING)

## SCHEDULE

05:00 - MORNING ROUTINE

06:00

07:00

08:00

09:00

10:00

11:00

12:00

13:00

14:00

15:00

16:00

17:00

18:00

19:00

20:00 - EVENING ROUTINE

# DAILY SELF CALL SHEET

DATE

M   T   W   T   F   S   S

## TOP THREE PRIORITIES

1.

2.

3.

## TODAY'S INNER MONOLOGUE MESSAGE

## TODAY'S HIGHLIGHT AHEAD

## TODAY'S ONE WORD OBJECTIVE

## POTENTIAL OBSTACLE

## HOW I CAN PREPARE FOR THIS

## A DIRECTOR WOULD REMIND ME

## I COULD CALL TODAY A SUCCESSFUL WRAP WHEN

## TODAY I AM GRATEFUL FOR

## REFLECT AND CELEBRATE (EVENING)

## SCHEDULE

05:00 - MORNING ROUTINE

06:00

07:00

08:00

09:00

10:00

11:00

12:00

13:00

14:00

15:00

16:00

17:00

18:00

19:00

20:00 - EVENING ROUTINE

# DAILY SELF CALL SHEET

DATE _____

M  T  W  T  F  S  S

## TOP THREE PRIORITIES

1. _____

2. _____

3. _____

## TODAY'S INNER MONOLOGUE MESSAGE

## TODAY'S HIGHLIGHT AHEAD

## TODAY'S ONE WORD OBJECTIVE

## POTENTIAL OBSTACLE

## HOW I CAN PREPARE FOR THIS

## A DIRECTOR WOULD REMIND ME

## I COULD CALL TODAY A SUCCESSFUL WRAP WHEN

## TODAY I AM GRATEFUL FOR

## REFLECT AND CELEBRATE (EVENING)

## SCHEDULE

05:00 - MORNING ROUTINE

06:00

07:00

08:00

09:00

10:00

11:00

12:00

13:00

14:00

15:00

16:00

17:00

18:00

19:00

20:00 - EVENING ROUTINE

# DAILY SELF CALL SHEET

DATE

M  T  W  T  F  S  S

## TOP THREE PRIORITIES

1.

2.

3.

## TODAY'S INNER MONOLOGUE MESSAGE

## TODAY'S HIGHLIGHT AHEAD

## TODAY'S ONE WORD OBJECTIVE

## POTENTIAL OBSTACLE

## HOW I CAN PREPARE FOR THIS

## A DIRECTOR WOULD REMIND ME

## I COULD CALL TODAY A SUCCESSFUL WRAP WHEN

## TODAY I AM GRATEFUL FOR

## REFLECT AND CELEBRATE (EVENING)

## SCHEDULE

05:00 - MORNING ROUTINE

06:00

07:00

08:00

09:00

10:00

11:00

12:00

13:00

14:00

15:00

16:00

17:00

18:00

19:00

20:00 - EVENING ROUTINE

# DAILY SELF CALL SHEET

DATE

M  T  W  T  F  S  S

## TOP THREE PRIORITIES

1.

2.

3.

## TODAY'S INNER MONOLOGUE MESSAGE

## TODAY'S HIGHLIGHT AHEAD

## TODAY'S ONE WORD OBJECTIVE

## POTENTIAL OBSTACLE

## HOW I CAN PREPARE FOR THIS

## A DIRECTOR WOULD REMIND ME

## I COULD CALL TODAY A SUCCESSFUL WRAP WHEN

## TODAY I AM GRATEFUL FOR

## REFLECT AND CELEBRATE (EVENING)

## SCHEDULE

05:00 - MORNING ROUTINE

06:00

07:00

08:00

09:00

10:00

11:00

12:00

13:00

14:00

15:00

16:00

17:00

18:00

19:00

20:00 - EVENING ROUTINE

# DIRECTOR'S CUT

**TOP THREE WINS THIS WEEK**

1. 

2. 

3. 

**WHAT DID I LEARN THIS WEEK**

**WHAT CAN I LET GO OF**

**WHAT WORKED WELL THIS WEEK**

**WHAT CAN I LOOK FORWARD TO**

**IS THERE ANYTHING I'M AVOIDING**

**HOW CAN I ACCOMPLISH THIS NEXT WEEK**

**WHAT'S MY BIGGEST PRIORITY THIS WEEK AHEAD**

**ADDITIONAL NOTES**

# DAILY SELF CALL SHEET

## TOP THREE PRIORITIES

1.

2.

3.

## TODAY'S INNER MONOLOGUE MESSAGE

## TODAY'S HIGHLIGHT AHEAD

## TODAY'S ONE WORD OBJECTIVE

## POTENTIAL OBSTACLE

## HOW I CAN PREPARE FOR THIS

## A DIRECTOR WOULD REMIND ME

## I COULD CALL TODAY A SUCCESSFUL WRAP WHEN

## TODAY I AM GRATEFUL FOR

## REFLECT AND CELEBRATE (EVENING)

## SCHEDULE

05:00 - MORNING ROUTINE

06:00

07:00

08:00

09:00

10:00

11:00

12:00

13:00

14:00

15:00

16:00

17:00

18:00

19:00

20:00 - EVENING ROUTINE

# DAILY SELF CALL SHEET

M  T  W  T  F  S  S

## TOP THREE PRIORITIES

1.

2.

3.

## TODAY'S INNER MONOLOGUE MESSAGE

## TODAY'S HIGHLIGHT AHEAD

## TODAY'S ONE WORD OBJECTIVE

## POTENTIAL OBSTACLE

## HOW I CAN PREPARE FOR THIS

## A DIRECTOR WOULD REMIND ME

## I COULD CALL TODAY A SUCCESSFUL WRAP WHEN

## TODAY I AM GRATEFUL FOR

## REFLECT AND CELEBRATE (EVENING)

## SCHEDULE

05:00 - MORNING ROUTINE

06:00

07:00

08:00

09:00

10:00

11:00

12:00

13:00

14:00

15:00

16:00

17:00

18:00

19:00

20:00 - EVENING ROUTINE

# DAILY SELF CALL SHEET

## TOP THREE PRIORITIES

1.

2.

3.

## TODAY'S INNER MONOLOGUE MESSAGE

## TODAY'S HIGHLIGHT AHEAD

## TODAY'S ONE WORD OBJECTIVE

## POTENTIAL OBSTACLE

## HOW I CAN PREPARE FOR THIS

## A DIRECTOR WOULD REMIND ME

## I COULD CALL TODAY A SUCCESSFUL WRAP WHEN

## TODAY I AM GRATEFUL FOR

## REFLECT AND CELEBRATE (EVENING)

## SCHEDULE

05:00 - MORNING ROUTINE

06:00

07:00

08:00

09:00

10:00

11:00

12:00

13:00

14:00

15:00

16:00

17:00

18:00

19:00

20:00 - EVENING ROUTINE

# DAILY SELF CALL SHEET

DATE

M  T  W  T  F  S  S

## TOP THREE PRIORITIES

1.

2.

3.

## TODAY'S INNER MONOLOGUE MESSAGE

## TODAY'S HIGHLIGHT AHEAD

## TODAY'S ONE WORD OBJECTIVE

## POTENTIAL OBSTACLE

## HOW I CAN PREPARE FOR THIS

## A DIRECTOR WOULD REMIND ME

## I COULD CALL TODAY A SUCCESSFUL WRAP WHEN

## TODAY I AM GRATEFUL FOR

## REFLECT AND CELEBRATE (EVENING)

## SCHEDULE

05:00 - MORNING ROUTINE

06:00

07:00

08:00

09:00

10:00

11:00

12:00

13:00

14:00

15:00

16:00

17:00

18:00

19:00

20:00 - EVENING ROUTINE

# DAILY SELF CALL SHEET

DATE

M  T  W  T  F  S  S

## TOP THREE PRIORITIES

1.

2.

3.

## TODAY'S INNER MONOLOGUE MESSAGE

## TODAY'S HIGHLIGHT AHEAD

## TODAY'S ONE WORD OBJECTIVE

## POTENTIAL OBSTACLE

## HOW I CAN PREPARE FOR THIS

## A DIRECTOR WOULD REMIND ME

## I COULD CALL TODAY A SUCCESSFUL WRAP WHEN

## TODAY I AM GRATEFUL FOR

## REFLECT AND CELEBRATE (EVENING)

## SCHEDULE

05:00 - MORNING ROUTINE

06:00

07:00

08:00

09:00

10:00

11:00

12:00

13:00

14:00

15:00

16:00

17:00

18:00

19:00

20:00 - EVENING ROUTINE

# DAILY SELF CALL SHEET

## TOP THREE PRIORITIES

1.

2.

3.

## TODAY'S INNER MONOLOGUE MESSAGE

## TODAY'S HIGHLIGHT AHEAD

## TODAY'S ONE WORD OBJECTIVE

## POTENTIAL OBSTACLE

## HOW I CAN PREPARE FOR THIS

## A DIRECTOR WOULD REMIND ME

## I COULD CALL TODAY A SUCCESSFUL WRAP WHEN

## TODAY I AM GRATEFUL FOR

## REFLECT AND CELEBRATE (EVENING)

## SCHEDULE

05:00 - MORNING ROUTINE

06:00

07:00

08:00

09:00

10:00

11:00

12:00

13:00

14:00

15:00

16:00

17:00

18:00

19:00

20:00 - EVENING ROUTINE

# DAILY SELF CALL SHEET

DATE

M  T  W  T  F  S  S

## TOP THREE PRIORITIES

1.

2.

3.

## TODAY'S INNER MONOLOGUE MESSAGE

## TODAY'S HIGHLIGHT AHEAD

## TODAY'S ONE WORD OBJECTIVE

## POTENTIAL OBSTACLE

## HOW I CAN PREPARE FOR THIS

## A DIRECTOR WOULD REMIND ME

## I COULD CALL TODAY A SUCCESSFUL WRAP WHEN

## TODAY I AM GRATEFUL FOR

## REFLECT AND CELEBRATE (EVENING)

## SCHEDULE

05:00 - MORNING ROUTINE

06:00

07:00

08:00

09:00

10:00

11:00

12:00

13:00

14:00

15:00

16:00

17:00

18:00

19:00

20:00 - EVENING ROUTINE

# DIRECTOR'S CUT

**TOP THREE WINS THIS WEEK**

1. _____

2. _____

3. _____

**WHAT DID I LEARN THIS WEEK**

**WHAT CAN I LET GO OF**

**WHAT WORKED WELL THIS WEEK**

**WHAT CAN I LOOK FORWARD TO**

**IS THERE ANYTHING I'M AVOIDING**

**HOW CAN I ACCOMPLISH THIS NEXT WEEK**

**WHAT'S MY BIGGEST PRIORITY THIS WEEK AHEAD**

**ADDITIONAL NOTES**

_____

_____

_____

_____

# DAILY SELF CALL SHEET

DATE _____

M  T  W  T  F  S  S

## TOP THREE PRIORITIES

1. _____

2. _____

3. _____

## TODAY'S INNER MONOLOGUE MESSAGE

## TODAY'S HIGHLIGHT AHEAD

## TODAY'S ONE WORD OBJECTIVE

## POTENTIAL OBSTACLE

## HOW I CAN PREPARE FOR THIS

## A DIRECTOR WOULD REMIND ME

## I COULD CALL TODAY A SUCCESSFUL WRAP WHEN

## TODAY I AM GRATEFUL FOR

## REFLECT AND CELEBRATE (EVENING)

## SCHEDULE

05:00 - MORNING ROUTINE

06:00

07:00

08:00

09:00

10:00

11:00

12:00

13:00

14:00

15:00

16:00

17:00

18:00

19:00

20:00 - EVENING ROUTINE

# DAILY SELF CALL SHEET

## TOP THREE PRIORITIES

1.

2.

3.

## TODAY'S INNER MONOLOGUE MESSAGE

## TODAY'S HIGHLIGHT AHEAD

## TODAY'S ONE WORD OBJECTIVE

## POTENTIAL OBSTACLE

## HOW I CAN PREPARE FOR THIS

## A DIRECTOR WOULD REMIND ME

## I COULD CALL TODAY A SUCCESSFUL WRAP WHEN

## TODAY I AM GRATEFUL FOR

## REFLECT AND CELEBRATE (EVENING)

## SCHEDULE

05:00 - MORNING ROUTINE

06:00

07:00

08:00

09:00

10:00

11:00

12:00

13:00

14:00

15:00

16:00

17:00

18:00

19:00

20:00 - EVENING ROUTINE

# DAILY SELF CALL SHEET

DATE

M   T   W   T   F   S   S

## TOP THREE PRIORITIES

1.

2.

3.

## TODAY'S INNER MONOLOGUE MESSAGE

## TODAY'S HIGHLIGHT AHEAD

## TODAY'S ONE WORD OBJECTIVE

## POTENTIAL OBSTACLE

## HOW I CAN PREPARE FOR THIS

## A DIRECTOR WOULD REMIND ME

## I COULD CALL TODAY A SUCCESSFUL WRAP WHEN

## TODAY I AM GRATEFUL FOR

## REFLECT AND CELEBRATE (EVENING)

## SCHEDULE

05:00 - MORNING ROUTINE

06:00

07:00

08:00

09:00

10:00

11:00

12:00

13:00

14:00

15:00

16:00

17:00

18:00

19:00

20:00 - EVENING ROUTINE

# DAILY SELF CALL SHEET

DATE

M  T  W  T  F  S  S

## TOP THREE PRIORITIES

1.

2.

3.

## TODAY'S INNER MONOLOGUE MESSAGE

## TODAY'S HIGHLIGHT AHEAD

## TODAY'S ONE WORD OBJECTIVE

## POTENTIAL OBSTACLE

## HOW I CAN PREPARE FOR THIS

## A DIRECTOR WOULD REMIND ME

## I COULD CALL TODAY A SUCCESSFUL WRAP WHEN

## TODAY I AM GRATEFUL FOR

## REFLECT AND CELEBRATE (EVENING)

## SCHEDULE

05:00 - MORNING ROUTINE

06:00

07:00

08:00

09:00

10:00

11:00

12:00

13:00

14:00

15:00

16:00

17:00

18:00

19:00

20:00 - EVENING ROUTINE

# DAILY SELF CALL SHEET

DATE

M  T  W  T  F  S  S

## TOP THREE PRIORITIES

1.

2.

3.

## TODAY'S INNER MONOLOGUE MESSAGE

## TODAY'S HIGHLIGHT AHEAD

## TODAY'S ONE WORD OBJECTIVE

## POTENTIAL OBSTACLE

## HOW I CAN PREPARE FOR THIS

## A DIRECTOR WOULD REMIND ME

## I COULD CALL TODAY A SUCCESSFUL WRAP WHEN

## TODAY I AM GRATEFUL FOR

## REFLECT AND CELEBRATE (EVENING)

## SCHEDULE

05:00 - MORNING ROUTINE

06:00

07:00

08:00

09:00

10:00

11:00

12:00

13:00

14:00

15:00

16:00

17:00

18:00

19:00

20:00 - EVENING ROUTINE

# DAILY SELF CALL SHEET

M    T    W    T    F    S    S

## TOP THREE PRIORITIES

1.

2.

3.

## TODAY'S INNER MONOLOGUE MESSAGE

## TODAY'S HIGHLIGHT AHEAD

## TODAY'S ONE WORD OBJECTIVE

## POTENTIAL OBSTACLE

## HOW I CAN PREPARE FOR THIS

## A DIRECTOR WOULD REMIND ME

## I COULD CALL TODAY A SUCCESSFUL WRAP WHEN

## TODAY I AM GRATEFUL FOR

## REFLECT AND CELEBRATE (EVENING)

## SCHEDULE

05:00 - MORNING ROUTINE

06:00

07:00

08:00

09:00

10:00

11:00

12:00

13:00

14:00

15:00

16:00

17:00

18:00

19:00

20:00 - EVENING ROUTINE

# DAILY SELF CALL SHEET

DATE _____

M  T  W  T  F  S  S

## TOP THREE PRIORITIES

1. _____

2. _____

3. _____

## TODAY'S INNER MONOLOGUE MESSAGE

## TODAY'S HIGHLIGHT AHEAD

## TODAY'S ONE WORD OBJECTIVE

## POTENTIAL OBSTACLE

## HOW I CAN PREPARE FOR THIS

## A DIRECTOR WOULD REMIND ME

## I COULD CALL TODAY A SUCCESSFUL WRAP WHEN

## TODAY I AM GRATEFUL FOR

## REFLECT AND CELEBRATE (EVENING)

## SCHEDULE

05:00 - MORNING ROUTINE

06:00

07:00

08:00

09:00

10:00

11:00

12:00

13:00

14:00

15:00

16:00

17:00

18:00

19:00

20:00 - EVENING ROUTINE

# DIRECTOR'S CUT

**TOP THREE WINS THIS WEEK**

1.

2.

3.

**WHAT DID I LEARN THIS WEEK**

**WHAT CAN I LET GO OF**

**WHAT WORKED WELL THIS WEEK**

**WHAT CAN I LOOK FORWARD TO**

**IS THERE ANYTHING I'M AVOIDING**

**HOW CAN I ACCOMPLISH THIS NEXT WEEK**

**WHAT'S MY BIGGEST PRIORITY THIS WEEK AHEAD**

**ADDITIONAL NOTES**

# DAILY SELF CALL SHEET

## TOP THREE PRIORITIES

1.

2.

3.

## TODAY'S INNER MONOLOGUE MESSAGE

## TODAY'S HIGHLIGHT AHEAD

## TODAY'S ONE WORD OBJECTIVE

## POTENTIAL OBSTACLE

## HOW I CAN PREPARE FOR THIS

## A DIRECTOR WOULD REMIND ME

## I COULD CALL TODAY A SUCCESSFUL WRAP WHEN

## TODAY I AM GRATEFUL FOR

## REFLECT AND CELEBRATE (EVENING)

## SCHEDULE

05:00 - MORNING ROUTINE

06:00

07:00

08:00

09:00

10:00

11:00

12:00

13:00

14:00

15:00

16:00

17:00

18:00

19:00

20:00 - EVENING ROUTINE

# DAILY SELF CALL SHEET

DATE

M  T  W  T  F  S  S

## TOP THREE PRIORITIES

1.

2.

3.

## TODAY'S INNER MONOLOGUE MESSAGE

## TODAY'S HIGHLIGHT AHEAD

## TODAY'S ONE WORD OBJECTIVE

## POTENTIAL OBSTACLE

## HOW I CAN PREPARE FOR THIS

## A DIRECTOR WOULD REMIND ME

## I COULD CALL TODAY A SUCCESSFUL WRAP WHEN

## TODAY I AM GRATEFUL FOR

## REFLECT AND CELEBRATE (EVENING)

## SCHEDULE

05:00 - MORNING ROUTINE

06:00

07:00

08:00

09:00

10:00

11:00

12:00

13:00

14:00

15:00

16:00

17:00

18:00

19:00

20:00 - EVENING ROUTINE

# DAILY SELF CALL SHEET

## TOP THREE PRIORITIES

1.

2.

3.

## TODAY'S INNER MONOLOGUE MESSAGE

## TODAY'S HIGHLIGHT AHEAD

## TODAY'S ONE WORD OBJECTIVE

## POTENTIAL OBSTACLE

## HOW I CAN PREPARE FOR THIS

## A DIRECTOR WOULD REMIND ME

## I COULD CALL TODAY A SUCCESSFUL WRAP WHEN

## TODAY I AM GRATEFUL FOR

## REFLECT AND CELEBRATE (EVENING)

## SCHEDULE

05:00 - MORNING ROUTINE

06:00

07:00

08:00

09:00

10:00

11:00

12:00

13:00

14:00

15:00

16:00

17:00

18:00

19:00

20:00 - EVENING ROUTINE

# DAILY SELF CALL SHEET

DATE

M  T  W  T  F  S  S

## TOP THREE PRIORITIES

1.

2.

3.

## TODAY'S INNER MONOLOGUE MESSAGE

## TODAY'S HIGHLIGHT AHEAD

## TODAY'S ONE WORD OBJECTIVE

## POTENTIAL OBSTACLE

## HOW I CAN PREPARE FOR THIS

## A DIRECTOR WOULD REMIND ME

## I COULD CALL TODAY A SUCCESSFUL WRAP WHEN

## TODAY I AM GRATEFUL FOR

## REFLECT AND CELEBRATE (EVENING)

## SCHEDULE

05:00 - MORNING ROUTINE

06:00

07:00

08:00

09:00

10:00

11:00

12:00

13:00

14:00

15:00

16:00

17:00

18:00

19:00

20:00 - EVENING ROUTINE

# DAILY SELF CALL SHEET

DATE

M T W T F S S

## TOP THREE PRIORITIES

1.

2.

3.

## TODAY'S INNER MONOLOGUE MESSAGE

## TODAY'S HIGHLIGHT AHEAD

## TODAY'S ONE WORD OBJECTIVE

## POTENTIAL OBSTACLE

## HOW I CAN PREPARE FOR THIS

## A DIRECTOR WOULD REMIND ME

## I COULD CALL TODAY A SUCCESSFUL WRAP WHEN

## TODAY I AM GRATEFUL FOR

## REFLECT AND CELEBRATE (EVENING)

## SCHEDULE

05:00 - MORNING ROUTINE

06:00

07:00

08:00

09:00

10:00

11:00

12:00

13:00

14:00

15:00

16:00

17:00

18:00

19:00

20:00 - EVENING ROUTINE

# DAILY SELF CALL SHEET

DATE _____

M  T  W  T  F  S  S

## TOP THREE PRIORITIES

1. _____

2. _____

3. _____

## TODAY'S INNER MONOLOGUE MESSAGE

## TODAY'S HIGHLIGHT AHEAD

## TODAY'S ONE WORD OBJECTIVE

## POTENTIAL OBSTACLE

## HOW I CAN PREPARE FOR THIS

## A DIRECTOR WOULD REMIND ME

## I COULD CALL TODAY A SUCCESSFUL WRAP WHEN

## TODAY I AM GRATEFUL FOR

## REFLECT AND CELEBRATE (EVENING)

## SCHEDULE

05:00 - MORNING ROUTINE

06:00

07:00

08:00

09:00

10:00

11:00

12:00

13:00

14:00

15:00

16:00

17:00

18:00

19:00

20:00 - EVENING ROUTINE

# DAILY SELF CALL SHEET

DATE _____

M   T   W   T   F   S   S

## TOP THREE PRIORITIES

1. _____

2. _____

3. _____

## TODAY'S INNER MONOLOGUE MESSAGE

## TODAY'S HIGHLIGHT AHEAD

## TODAY'S ONE WORD OBJECTIVE

## POTENTIAL OBSTACLE

## HOW I CAN PREPARE FOR THIS

## A DIRECTOR WOULD REMIND ME

## I COULD CALL TODAY A SUCCESSFUL WRAP WHEN

## TODAY I AM GRATEFUL FOR

## REFLECT AND CELEBRATE (EVENING)

## SCHEDULE

05:00 - MORNING ROUTINE

06:00

07:00

08:00

09:00

10:00

11:00

12:00

13:00

14:00

15:00

16:00

17:00

18:00

19:00

20:00 - EVENING ROUTINE

# DIRECTOR'S CUT

## TOP THREE WINS THIS WEEK

1. _____

2. _____

3. _____

## WHAT DID I LEARN THIS WEEK

## WHAT CAN I LET GO OF

## WHAT WORKED WELL THIS WEEK

## WHAT CAN I LOOK FORWARD TO

## IS THERE ANYTHING I'M AVOIDING

## HOW CAN I ACCOMPLISH THIS NEXT WEEK

## WHAT'S MY BIGGEST PRIORITY THIS WEEK AHEAD

## ADDITIONAL NOTES

_____

_____

_____

# DAILY SELF CALL SHEET

DATE

M  T  W  T  F  S  S

## TOP THREE PRIORITIES

1.

2.

3.

## TODAY'S INNER MONOLOGUE MESSAGE

## TODAY'S HIGHLIGHT AHEAD

## TODAY'S ONE WORD OBJECTIVE

## POTENTIAL OBSTACLE

## HOW I CAN PREPARE FOR THIS

## A DIRECTOR WOULD REMIND ME

## I COULD CALL TODAY A SUCCESSFUL WRAP WHEN

## TODAY I AM GRATEFUL FOR

## REFLECT AND CELEBRATE (EVENING)

## SCHEDULE

05:00 - MORNING ROUTINE

06:00

07:00

08:00

09:00

10:00

11:00

12:00

13:00

14:00

15:00

16:00

17:00

18:00

19:00

20:00 - EVENING ROUTINE

# DAILY SELF CALL SHEET

DATE

M  T  W  T  F  S  S

## TOP THREE PRIORITIES

1.

2.

3.

## TODAY'S INNER MONOLOGUE MESSAGE

## TODAY'S HIGHLIGHT AHEAD

## TODAY'S ONE WORD OBJECTIVE

## POTENTIAL OBSTACLE

## HOW I CAN PREPARE FOR THIS

## A DIRECTOR WOULD REMIND ME

## I COULD CALL TODAY A SUCCESSFUL WRAP WHEN

## TODAY I AM GRATEFUL FOR

## REFLECT AND CELEBRATE (EVENING)

## SCHEDULE

05:00 - MORNING ROUTINE

06:00

07:00

08:00

09:00

10:00

11:00

12:00

13:00

14:00

15:00

16:00

17:00

18:00

19:00

20:00 - EVENING ROUTINE

# DAILY SELF CALL SHEET

DATE

M  T  W  T  F  S  S

## TOP THREE PRIORITIES

1.

2.

3.

## TODAY'S INNER MONOLOGUE MESSAGE

## TODAY'S HIGHLIGHT AHEAD

## TODAY'S ONE WORD OBJECTIVE

## POTENTIAL OBSTACLE

## HOW I CAN PREPARE FOR THIS

## A DIRECTOR WOULD REMIND ME

## I COULD CALL TODAY A SUCCESSFUL WRAP WHEN

## TODAY I AM GRATEFUL FOR

## REFLECT AND CELEBRATE (EVENING)

## SCHEDULE

05:00 - MORNING ROUTINE

06:00

07:00

08:00

09:00

10:00

11:00

12:00

13:00

14:00

15:00

16:00

17:00

18:00

19:00

20:00 - EVENING ROUTINE

# DAILY SELF CALL SHEET

DATE _____

M  T  W  T  F  S  S

## TOP THREE PRIORITIES

1. _____

2. _____

3. _____

## TODAY'S INNER MONOLOGUE MESSAGE

## TODAY'S HIGHLIGHT AHEAD

## TODAY'S ONE WORD OBJECTIVE

## POTENTIAL OBSTACLE

## HOW I CAN PREPARE FOR THIS

## A DIRECTOR WOULD REMIND ME

## I COULD CALL TODAY A SUCCESSFUL WRAP WHEN

## TODAY I AM GRATEFUL FOR

## REFLECT AND CELEBRATE (EVENING)

## SCHEDULE

05:00 - MORNING ROUTINE

06:00

07:00

08:00

09:00

10:00

11:00

12:00

13:00

14:00

15:00

16:00

17:00

18:00

19:00

20:00 - EVENING ROUTINE

# DAILY SELF CALL SHEET

M  T  W  T  F  S  S

## TOP THREE PRIORITIES

1.

2.

3.

## TODAY'S INNER MONOLOGUE MESSAGE

## TODAY'S HIGHLIGHT AHEAD

## TODAY'S ONE WORD OBJECTIVE

## POTENTIAL OBSTACLE

## HOW I CAN PREPARE FOR THIS

## A DIRECTOR WOULD REMIND ME

## I COULD CALL TODAY A SUCCESSFUL WRAP WHEN

## TODAY I AM GRATEFUL FOR

## REFLECT AND CELEBRATE (EVENING)

## SCHEDULE

05:00 - MORNING ROUTINE

06:00

07:00

08:00

09:00

10:00

11:00

12:00

13:00

14:00

15:00

16:00

17:00

18:00

19:00

20:00 - EVENING ROUTINE

# DAILY SELF CALL SHEET

DATE

M  T  W  T  F  S  S

## TOP THREE PRIORITIES

1.

2.

3.

## TODAY'S INNER MONOLOGUE MESSAGE

## TODAY'S HIGHLIGHT AHEAD

## TODAY'S ONE WORD OBJECTIVE

## POTENTIAL OBSTACLE

## HOW I CAN PREPARE FOR THIS

## A DIRECTOR WOULD REMIND ME

## I COULD CALL TODAY A SUCCESSFUL WRAP WHEN

## TODAY I AM GRATEFUL FOR

## REFLECT AND CELEBRATE (EVENING)

## SCHEDULE

05:00 - MORNING ROUTINE

06:00

07:00

08:00

09:00

10:00

11:00

12:00

13:00

14:00

15:00

16:00

17:00

18:00

19:00

20:00 - EVENING ROUTINE

# DAILY SELF CALL SHEET

DATE

M  T  W  T  F  S  S

## TOP THREE PRIORITIES

1.

2.

3.

## TODAY'S INNER MONOLOGUE MESSAGE

## TODAY'S HIGHLIGHT AHEAD

## TODAY'S ONE WORD OBJECTIVE

## POTENTIAL OBSTACLE

## HOW I CAN PREPARE FOR THIS

## A DIRECTOR WOULD REMIND ME

## I COULD CALL TODAY A SUCCESSFUL WRAP WHEN

## TODAY I AM GRATEFUL FOR

## REFLECT AND CELEBRATE (EVENING)

## SCHEDULE

05:00 - MORNING ROUTINE

06:00

07:00

08:00

09:00

10:00

11:00

12:00

13:00

14:00

15:00

16:00

17:00

18:00

19:00

20:00 - EVENING ROUTINE

# DIRECTOR'S CUT

**TOP THREE WINS THIS WEEK**

1. 

2. 

3. 

**WHAT DID I LEARN THIS WEEK**

**WHAT CAN I LET GO OF**

**WHAT WORKED WELL THIS WEEK**

**WHAT CAN I LOOK FORWARD TO**

**IS THERE ANYTHING I'M AVOIDING**

**HOW CAN I ACCOMPLISH THIS NEXT WEEK**

**WHAT'S MY BIGGEST PRIORITY THIS WEEK AHEAD**

**ADDITIONAL NOTES**

# DAILY SELF CALL SHEET

DATE _____

M  T  W  T  F  S  S

## TOP THREE PRIORITIES

1. _____

2. _____

3. _____

## TODAY'S INNER MONOLOGUE MESSAGE

## TODAY'S HIGHLIGHT AHEAD

## TODAY'S ONE WORD OBJECTIVE

## POTENTIAL OBSTACLE

## HOW I CAN PREPARE FOR THIS

## A DIRECTOR WOULD REMIND ME

## I COULD CALL TODAY A SUCCESSFUL WRAP WHEN

## TODAY I AM GRATEFUL FOR

## REFLECT AND CELEBRATE (EVENING)

## SCHEDULE

05:00 - MORNING ROUTINE

06:00

07:00

08:00

09:00

10:00

11:00

12:00

13:00

14:00

15:00

16:00

17:00

18:00

19:00

20:00 - EVENING ROUTINE

# DAILY SELF CALL SHEET

DATE

M   T   W   T   F   S   S

## TOP THREE PRIORITIES

1.

2.

3.

## TODAY'S INNER MONOLOGUE MESSAGE

## TODAY'S HIGHLIGHT AHEAD

## TODAY'S ONE WORD OBJECTIVE

## POTENTIAL OBSTACLE

## HOW I CAN PREPARE FOR THIS

## A DIRECTOR WOULD REMIND ME

## I COULD CALL TODAY A SUCCESSFUL WRAP WHEN

## TODAY I AM GRATEFUL FOR

## REFLECT AND CELEBRATE (EVENING)

## SCHEDULE

05:00 - MORNING ROUTINE

06:00

07:00

08:00

09:00

10:00

11:00

12:00

13:00

14:00

15:00

16:00

17:00

18:00

19:00

20:00 - EVENING ROUTINE

# DAILY SELF CALL SHEET

DATE

M  T  W  T  F  S  S

## TOP THREE PRIORITIES

1.

2.

3.

## TODAY'S INNER MONOLOGUE MESSAGE

## TODAY'S HIGHLIGHT AHEAD

## TODAY'S ONE WORD OBJECTIVE

## POTENTIAL OBSTACLE

## HOW I CAN PREPARE FOR THIS

## A DIRECTOR WOULD REMIND ME

## I COULD CALL TODAY A SUCCESSFUL WRAP WHEN

## TODAY I AM GRATEFUL FOR

## REFLECT AND CELEBRATE (EVENING)

## SCHEDULE

05:00 - MORNING ROUTINE

06:00

07:00

08:00

09:00

10:00

11:00

12:00

13:00

14:00

15:00

16:00

17:00

18:00

19:00

20:00 - EVENING ROUTINE

# DAILY SELF CALL SHEET

DATE _____

M   T   W   T   F   S   S

## TOP THREE PRIORITIES

1. _____

2. _____

3. _____

## TODAY'S INNER MONOLOGUE MESSAGE

## TODAY'S HIGHLIGHT AHEAD

## TODAY'S ONE WORD OBJECTIVE

## POTENTIAL OBSTACLE

## HOW I CAN PREPARE FOR THIS

## A DIRECTOR WOULD REMIND ME

## I COULD CALL TODAY A SUCCESSFUL WRAP WHEN

## TODAY I AM GRATEFUL FOR

## REFLECT AND CELEBRATE (EVENING)

## SCHEDULE

05:00 - MORNING ROUTINE

06:00

07:00

08:00

09:00

10:00

11:00

12:00

13:00

14:00

15:00

16:00

17:00

18:00

19:00

20:00 - EVENING ROUTINE

# DAILY SELF CALL SHEET

DATE _____

M   T   W   T   F   S   S

## TOP THREE PRIORITIES

1. _____

2. _____

3. _____

## TODAY'S INNER MONOLOGUE MESSAGE

## TODAY'S HIGHLIGHT AHEAD

## TODAY'S ONE WORD OBJECTIVE

## POTENTIAL OBSTACLE

## HOW I CAN PREPARE FOR THIS

## A DIRECTOR WOULD REMIND ME

## I COULD CALL TODAY A SUCCESSFUL WRAP WHEN

## TODAY I AM GRATEFUL FOR

## REFLECT AND CELEBRATE (EVENING)

## SCHEDULE

05:00 - MORNING ROUTINE

06:00

07:00

08:00

09:00

10:00

11:00

12:00

13:00

14:00

15:00

16:00

17:00

18:00

19:00

20:00 - EVENING ROUTINE

# DAILY SELF CALL SHEET

DATE

M   T   W   T   F   S   S

## TOP THREE PRIORITIES

1.

2.

3.

## TODAY'S INNER MONOLOGUE MESSAGE

## TODAY'S HIGHLIGHT AHEAD

## TODAY'S ONE WORD OBJECTIVE

## POTENTIAL OBSTACLE

## HOW I CAN PREPARE FOR THIS

## A DIRECTOR WOULD REMIND ME

## I COULD CALL TODAY A SUCCESSFUL WRAP WHEN

## TODAY I AM GRATEFUL FOR

## REFLECT AND CELEBRATE (EVENING)

## SCHEDULE

05:00 - MORNING ROUTINE

06:00

07:00

08:00

09:00

10:00

11:00

12:00

13:00

14:00

15:00

16:00

17:00

18:00

19:00

20:00 - EVENING ROUTINE

# DAILY SELF CALL SHEET

## TOP THREE PRIORITIES

1.

2.

3.

## TODAY'S INNER MONOLOGUE MESSAGE

## TODAY'S HIGHLIGHT AHEAD

## TODAY'S ONE WORD OBJECTIVE

## POTENTIAL OBSTACLE

## HOW I CAN PREPARE FOR THIS

## A DIRECTOR WOULD REMIND ME

## I COULD CALL TODAY A SUCCESSFUL WRAP WHEN

## TODAY I AM GRATEFUL FOR

## REFLECT AND CELEBRATE (EVENING)

## SCHEDULE

05:00 - MORNING ROUTINE

06:00

07:00

08:00

09:00

10:00

11:00

12:00

13:00

14:00

15:00

16:00

17:00

18:00

19:00

20:00 - EVENING ROUTINE

# DIRECTOR'S CUT

TOP THREE WINS THIS WEEK

1.

2.

3.

WHAT DID I LEARN THIS WEEK

WHAT CAN I LET GO OF

WHAT WORKED WELL THIS WEEK

WHAT CAN I LOOK FORWARD TO

IS THERE ANYTHING I'M AVOIDING

HOW CAN I ACCOMPLISH THIS NEXT WEEK

WHAT'S MY BIGGEST PRIORITY THIS WEEK AHEAD

ADDITIONAL NOTES

# DAILY SELF CALL SHEET

DATE _____

M   T   W   T   F   S   S

## TOP THREE PRIORITIES

1. _____
2. _____
3. _____

## TODAY'S INNER MONOLOGUE MESSAGE

## TODAY'S HIGHLIGHT AHEAD

## TODAY'S ONE WORD OBJECTIVE

## POTENTIAL OBSTACLE

## HOW I CAN PREPARE FOR THIS

## A DIRECTOR WOULD REMIND ME

## I COULD CALL TODAY A SUCCESSFUL WRAP WHEN

## TODAY I AM GRATEFUL FOR

## REFLECT AND CELEBRATE (EVENING)

## SCHEDULE

05:00 - MORNING ROUTINE

06:00

07:00

08:00

09:00

10:00

11:00

12:00

13:00

14:00

15:00

16:00

17:00

18:00

19:00

20:00 - EVENING ROUTINE

# DAILY SELF CALL SHEET

DATE

M  T  W  T  F  S  S

## TOP THREE PRIORITIES

1.

2.

3.

## TODAY'S INNER MONOLOGUE MESSAGE

## TODAY'S HIGHLIGHT AHEAD

## TODAY'S ONE WORD OBJECTIVE

## POTENTIAL OBSTACLE

## HOW I CAN PREPARE FOR THIS

## A DIRECTOR WOULD REMIND ME

## I COULD CALL TODAY A SUCCESSFUL WRAP WHEN

## TODAY I AM GRATEFUL FOR

## REFLECT AND CELEBRATE (EVENING)

## SCHEDULE

05:00 - MORNING ROUTINE

06:00

07:00

08:00

09:00

10:00

11:00

12:00

13:00

14:00

15:00

16:00

17:00

18:00

19:00

20:00 - EVENING ROUTINE

# DAILY SELF CALL SHEET

## TOP THREE PRIORITIES

1.

2.

3.

## TODAY'S INNER MONOLOGUE MESSAGE

## TODAY'S HIGHLIGHT AHEAD

## TODAY'S ONE WORD OBJECTIVE

## POTENTIAL OBSTACLE

## HOW I CAN PREPARE FOR THIS

## A DIRECTOR WOULD REMIND ME

## I COULD CALL TODAY A SUCCESSFUL WRAP WHEN

## TODAY I AM GRATEFUL FOR

## REFLECT AND CELEBRATE (EVENING)

## SCHEDULE

05:00 - MORNING ROUTINE

06:00

07:00

08:00

09:00

10:00

11:00

12:00

13:00

14:00

15:00

16:00

17:00

18:00

19:00

20:00 - EVENING ROUTINE

# DAILY SELF CALL SHEET

DATE

M  T  W  T  F  S  S

## TOP THREE PRIORITIES

1.

2.

3.

## TODAY'S INNER MONOLOGUE MESSAGE

## TODAY'S HIGHLIGHT AHEAD

## TODAY'S ONE WORD OBJECTIVE

## POTENTIAL OBSTACLE

## HOW I CAN PREPARE FOR THIS

## A DIRECTOR WOULD REMIND ME

## I COULD CALL TODAY A SUCCESSFUL WRAP WHEN

## TODAY I AM GRATEFUL FOR

## REFLECT AND CELEBRATE (EVENING)

## SCHEDULE

05:00 - MORNING ROUTINE

06:00

07:00

08:00

09:00

10:00

11:00

12:00

13:00

14:00

15:00

16:00

17:00

18:00

19:00

20:00 - EVENING ROUTINE

# DAILY SELF CALL SHEET

DATE _____

M  T  W  T  F  S  S

## TOP THREE PRIORITIES

1. _____

2. _____

3. _____

## TODAY'S INNER MONOLOGUE MESSAGE

## TODAY'S HIGHLIGHT AHEAD

## TODAY'S ONE WORD OBJECTIVE

## POTENTIAL OBSTACLE

## HOW I CAN PREPARE FOR THIS

## A DIRECTOR WOULD REMIND ME

## I COULD CALL TODAY A SUCCESSFUL WRAP WHEN

## TODAY I AM GRATEFUL FOR

## REFLECT AND CELEBRATE (EVENING)

## SCHEDULE

05:00 - MORNING ROUTINE

06:00

07:00

08:00

09:00

10:00

11:00

12:00

13:00

14:00

15:00

16:00

17:00

18:00

19:00

20:00 - EVENING ROUTINE

# DAILY SELF CALL SHEET

## TOP THREE PRIORITIES

1.

2.

3.

## TODAY'S INNER MONOLOGUE MESSAGE

## TODAY'S HIGHLIGHT AHEAD

## TODAY'S ONE WORD OBJECTIVE

## POTENTIAL OBSTACLE

## HOW I CAN PREPARE FOR THIS

## A DIRECTOR WOULD REMIND ME

## I COULD CALL TODAY A SUCCESSFUL WRAP WHEN

## TODAY I AM GRATEFUL FOR

## REFLECT AND CELEBRATE (EVENING)

## SCHEDULE

05:00 - MORNING ROUTINE

06:00

07:00

08:00

09:00

10:00

11:00

12:00

13:00

14:00

15:00

16:00

17:00

18:00

19:00

20:00 - EVENING ROUTINE

# DAILY SELF CALL SHEET

DATE

## TOP THREE PRIORITIES

1.

2.

3.

## TODAY'S INNER MONOLOGUE MESSAGE

## TODAY'S HIGHLIGHT AHEAD

## TODAY'S ONE WORD OBJECTIVE

## POTENTIAL OBSTACLE

## HOW I CAN PREPARE FOR THIS

## A DIRECTOR WOULD REMIND ME

## I COULD CALL TODAY A SUCCESSFUL WRAP WHEN

## TODAY I AM GRATEFUL FOR

## REFLECT AND CELEBRATE (EVENING)

## SCHEDULE

05:00 - MORNING ROUTINE

06:00

07:00

08:00

09:00

10:00

11:00

12:00

13:00

14:00

15:00

16:00

17:00

18:00

19:00

20:00 - EVENING ROUTINE

# DIRECTOR'S CUT

**TOP THREE WINS THIS WEEK**

1.

2.

3.

**WHAT DID I LEARN THIS WEEK**

**WHAT CAN I LET GO OF**

**WHAT WORKED WELL THIS WEEK**

**WHAT CAN I LOOK FORWARD TO**

**IS THERE ANYTHING I'M AVOIDING**

**HOW CAN I ACCOMPLISH THIS NEXT WEEK**

**WHAT'S MY BIGGEST PRIORITY THIS WEEK AHEAD**

**ADDITIONAL NOTES**

# DAILY SELF CALL SHEET

DATE _____

M  T  W  T  F  S  S

## TOP THREE PRIORITIES

1. _____

2. _____

3. _____

### TODAY'S INNER MONOLOGUE MESSAGE

### TODAY'S HIGHLIGHT AHEAD

### TODAY'S ONE WORD OBJECTIVE

### POTENTIAL OBSTACLE

### HOW I CAN PREPARE FOR THIS

### A DIRECTOR WOULD REMIND ME

### I COULD CALL TODAY A SUCCESSFUL WRAP WHEN

### TODAY I AM GRATEFUL FOR

### REFLECT AND CELEBRATE (EVENING)

## SCHEDULE

05:00 - MORNING ROUTINE

06:00

07:00

08:00

09:00

10:00

11:00

12:00

13:00

14:00

15:00

16:00

17:00

18:00

19:00

20:00 - EVENING ROUTINE

# DAILY SELF CALL SHEET

DATE

M  T  W  T  F  S  S

## TOP THREE PRIORITIES

1.

2.

3.

## TODAY'S INNER MONOLOGUE MESSAGE

## TODAY'S HIGHLIGHT AHEAD

## TODAY'S ONE WORD OBJECTIVE

## POTENTIAL OBSTACLE

## HOW I CAN PREPARE FOR THIS

## A DIRECTOR WOULD REMIND ME

## I COULD CALL TODAY A SUCCESSFUL WRAP WHEN

## TODAY I AM GRATEFUL FOR

## REFLECT AND CELEBRATE (EVENING)

## SCHEDULE

05:00 - MORNING ROUTINE

06:00

07:00

08:00

09:00

10:00

11:00

12:00

13:00

14:00

15:00

16:00

17:00

18:00

19:00

20:00 - EVENING ROUTINE

# DAILY SELF CALL SHEET

DATE

M  T  W  T  F  S  S

## TOP THREE PRIORITIES

1.

2.

3.

## TODAY'S INNER MONOLOGUE MESSAGE

## TODAY'S HIGHLIGHT AHEAD

## TODAY'S ONE WORD OBJECTIVE

## POTENTIAL OBSTACLE

## HOW I CAN PREPARE FOR THIS

## A DIRECTOR WOULD REMIND ME

## I COULD CALL TODAY A SUCCESSFUL WRAP WHEN

## TODAY I AM GRATEFUL FOR

## REFLECT AND CELEBRATE (EVENING)

## SCHEDULE

05:00 - MORNING ROUTINE

06:00

07:00

08:00

09:00

10:00

11:00

12:00

13:00

14:00

15:00

16:00

17:00

18:00

19:00

20:00 - EVENING ROUTINE

# DAILY SELF CALL SHEET

DATE

M   T   W   T   F   S   S

## TOP THREE PRIORITIES

1.

2.

3.

## TODAY'S INNER MONOLOGUE MESSAGE

## TODAY'S HIGHLIGHT AHEAD

## TODAY'S ONE WORD OBJECTIVE

## POTENTIAL OBSTACLE

## HOW I CAN PREPARE FOR THIS

## A DIRECTOR WOULD REMIND ME

## I COULD CALL TODAY A SUCCESSFUL WRAP WHEN

## TODAY I AM GRATEFUL FOR

## REFLECT AND CELEBRATE (EVENING)

## SCHEDULE

05:00 - MORNING ROUTINE

06:00

07:00

08:00

09:00

10:00

11:00

12:00

13:00

14:00

15:00

16:00

17:00

18:00

19:00

20:00 - EVENING ROUTINE

# DAILY SELF CALL SHEET

## TOP THREE PRIORITIES

1.

2.

3.

## TODAY'S INNER MONOLOGUE MESSAGE

## TODAY'S HIGHLIGHT AHEAD

## TODAY'S ONE WORD OBJECTIVE

## POTENTIAL OBSTACLE

## HOW I CAN PREPARE FOR THIS

## A DIRECTOR WOULD REMIND ME

## I COULD CALL TODAY A SUCCESSFUL WRAP WHEN

## TODAY I AM GRATEFUL FOR

## REFLECT AND CELEBRATE (EVENING)

## SCHEDULE

05:00 - MORNING ROUTINE

06:00

07:00

08:00

09:00

10:00

11:00

12:00

13:00

14:00

15:00

16:00

17:00

18:00

19:00

20:00 - EVENING ROUTINE

# DAILY SELF CALL SHEET

DATE

M  T  W  T  F  S  S

## TOP THREE PRIORITIES

1.

2.

3.

## TODAY'S INNER MONOLOGUE MESSAGE

## TODAY'S HIGHLIGHT AHEAD

## TODAY'S ONE WORD OBJECTIVE

## POTENTIAL OBSTACLE

## HOW I CAN PREPARE FOR THIS

## A DIRECTOR WOULD REMIND ME

## I COULD CALL TODAY A SUCCESSFUL WRAP WHEN

## TODAY I AM GRATEFUL FOR

## REFLECT AND CELEBRATE (EVENING)

## SCHEDULE

05:00 - MORNING ROUTINE

06:00

07:00

08:00

09:00

10:00

11:00

12:00

13:00

14:00

15:00

16:00

17:00

18:00

19:00

20:00 - EVENING ROUTINE

# DAILY SELF CALL SHEET

## TOP THREE PRIORITIES

1.

2.

3.

## TODAY'S INNER MONOLOGUE MESSAGE

## TODAY'S HIGHLIGHT AHEAD

## TODAY'S ONE WORD OBJECTIVE

## POTENTIAL OBSTACLE

## HOW I CAN PREPARE FOR THIS

## A DIRECTOR WOULD REMIND ME

## I COULD CALL TODAY A SUCCESSFUL WRAP WHEN

## TODAY I AM GRATEFUL FOR

## REFLECT AND CELEBRATE (EVENING)

## SCHEDULE

05:00 - MORNING ROUTINE

06:00

07:00

08:00

09:00

10:00

11:00

12:00

13:00

14:00

15:00

16:00

17:00

18:00

19:00

20:00 - EVENING ROUTINE

# DIRECTOR'S CUT

**TOP THREE WINS THIS WEEK**

1. _____

2. _____

3. _____

**WHAT DID I LEARN THIS WEEK**

**WHAT CAN I LET GO OF**

**WHAT WORKED WELL THIS WEEK**

**WHAT CAN I LOOK FORWARD TO**

**IS THERE ANYTHING I'M AVOIDING**

**HOW CAN I ACCOMPLISH THIS NEXT WEEK**

**WHAT'S MY BIGGEST PRIORITY THIS WEEK AHEAD**

**ADDITIONAL NOTES**

_____

_____

_____

# DAILY SELF CALL SHEET

## TOP THREE PRIORITIES

1.

2.

3.

## TODAY'S INNER MONOLOGUE MESSAGE

## TODAY'S HIGHLIGHT AHEAD

## TODAY'S ONE WORD OBJECTIVE

## POTENTIAL OBSTACLE

## HOW I CAN PREPARE FOR THIS

## A DIRECTOR WOULD REMIND ME

## I COULD CALL TODAY A SUCCESSFUL WRAP WHEN

## TODAY I AM GRATEFUL FOR

## REFLECT AND CELEBRATE (EVENING)

## SCHEDULE

05:00 - MORNING ROUTINE

06:00

07:00

08:00

09:00

10:00

11:00

12:00

13:00

14:00

15:00

16:00

17:00

18:00

19:00

20:00 - EVENING ROUTINE

# DAILY SELF CALL SHEET

DATE

M  T  W  T  F  S  S

## TOP THREE PRIORITIES

1.

2.

3.

## TODAY'S INNER MONOLOGUE MESSAGE

## TODAY'S HIGHLIGHT AHEAD

## TODAY'S ONE WORD OBJECTIVE

## POTENTIAL OBSTACLE

## HOW I CAN PREPARE FOR THIS

## A DIRECTOR WOULD REMIND ME

## I COULD CALL TODAY A SUCCESSFUL WRAP WHEN

## TODAY I AM GRATEFUL FOR

## REFLECT AND CELEBRATE (EVENING)

## SCHEDULE

05:00 - MORNING ROUTINE

06:00

07:00

08:00

09:00

10:00

11:00

12:00

13:00

14:00

15:00

16:00

17:00

18:00

19:00

20:00 - EVENING ROUTINE

# DAILY SELF CALL SHEET

DATE

M T W T F S S

## TOP THREE PRIORITIES

1.

2.

3.

## TODAY'S INNER MONOLOGUE MESSAGE

## TODAY'S HIGHLIGHT AHEAD

## TODAY'S ONE WORD OBJECTIVE

## POTENTIAL OBSTACLE

## HOW I CAN PREPARE FOR THIS

## A DIRECTOR WOULD REMIND ME

## I COULD CALL TODAY A SUCCESSFUL WRAP WHEN

## TODAY I AM GRATEFUL FOR

## REFLECT AND CELEBRATE (EVENING)

## SCHEDULE

05:00 - MORNING ROUTINE

06:00

07:00

08:00

09:00

10:00

11:00

12:00

13:00

14:00

15:00

16:00

17:00

18:00

19:00

20:00 - EVENING ROUTINE

# DAILY SELF CALL SHEET

DATE

M  T  W  T  F  S  S

## TOP THREE PRIORITIES

1.

2.

3.

## TODAY'S INNER MONOLOGUE MESSAGE

## TODAY'S HIGHLIGHT AHEAD

## TODAY'S ONE WORD OBJECTIVE

## POTENTIAL OBSTACLE

## HOW I CAN PREPARE FOR THIS

## A DIRECTOR WOULD REMIND ME

## I COULD CALL TODAY A SUCCESSFUL WRAP WHEN

## TODAY I AM GRATEFUL FOR

## REFLECT AND CELEBRATE (EVENING)

## SCHEDULE

05:00 - MORNING ROUTINE

06:00

07:00

08:00

09:00

10:00

11:00

12:00

13:00

14:00

15:00

16:00

17:00

18:00

19:00

20:00 - EVENING ROUTINE

# DAILY SELF CALL SHEET

DATE

M  T  W  T  F  S  S

## TOP THREE PRIORITIES

1.

2.

3.

## TODAY'S INNER MONOLOGUE MESSAGE

## TODAY'S HIGHLIGHT AHEAD

## TODAY'S ONE WORD OBJECTIVE

## POTENTIAL OBSTACLE

## HOW I CAN PREPARE FOR THIS

## A DIRECTOR WOULD REMIND ME

## I COULD CALL TODAY A SUCCESSFUL WRAP WHEN

## TODAY I AM GRATEFUL FOR

## REFLECT AND CELEBRATE (EVENING)

## SCHEDULE

05:00 - MORNING ROUTINE

06:00

07:00

08:00

09:00

10:00

11:00

12:00

13:00

14:00

15:00

16:00

17:00

18:00

19:00

20:00 - EVENING ROUTINE

# DAILY SELF CALL SHEET

DATE _____

M  T  W  T  F  S  S

## TOP THREE PRIORITIES

1. _____
2. _____
3. _____

## TODAY'S INNER MONOLOGUE MESSAGE

## TODAY'S HIGHLIGHT AHEAD

## TODAY'S ONE WORD OBJECTIVE

## POTENTIAL OBSTACLE

## HOW I CAN PREPARE FOR THIS

## A DIRECTOR WOULD REMIND ME

## I COULD CALL TODAY A SUCCESSFUL WRAP WHEN

## TODAY I AM GRATEFUL FOR

## REFLECT AND CELEBRATE (EVENING)

## SCHEDULE

05:00 - MORNING ROUTINE

06:00

07:00

08:00

09:00

10:00

11:00

12:00

13:00

14:00

15:00

16:00

17:00

18:00

19:00

20:00 - EVENING ROUTINE

# DAILY SELF CALL SHEET

DATE _____

M   T   W   T   F   S   S

## TOP THREE PRIORITIES

1. _____

2. _____

3. _____

## TODAY'S INNER MONOLOGUE MESSAGE

## TODAY'S HIGHLIGHT AHEAD

## TODAY'S ONE WORD OBJECTIVE

## POTENTIAL OBSTACLE

## HOW I CAN PREPARE FOR THIS

## A DIRECTOR WOULD REMIND ME

## I COULD CALL TODAY A SUCCESSFUL WRAP WHEN

## TODAY I AM GRATEFUL FOR

## REFLECT AND CELEBRATE (EVENING)

## SCHEDULE

05:00 - MORNING ROUTINE

06:00

07:00

08:00

09:00

10:00

11:00

12:00

13:00

14:00

15:00

16:00

17:00

18:00

19:00

20:00 - EVENING ROUTINE

# DIRECTOR'S CUT

## TOP THREE WINS THIS WEEK

1.

2.

3.

## WHAT DID I LEARN THIS WEEK

## WHAT CAN I LET GO OF

## WHAT WORKED WELL THIS WEEK

## WHAT CAN I LOOK FORWARD TO

## IS THERE ANYTHING I'M AVOIDING

## HOW CAN I ACCOMPLISH THIS NEXT WEEK

## WHAT'S MY BIGGEST PRIORITY THIS WEEK AHEAD

## ADDITIONAL NOTES

# DAILY SELF CALL SHEET

DATE

M  T  W  T  F  S  S

## TOP THREE PRIORITIES

1.

2.

3.

## TODAY'S INNER MONOLOGUE MESSAGE

## TODAY'S HIGHLIGHT AHEAD

## TODAY'S ONE WORD OBJECTIVE

## POTENTIAL OBSTACLE

## HOW I CAN PREPARE FOR THIS

## A DIRECTOR WOULD REMIND ME

## I COULD CALL TODAY A SUCCESSFUL WRAP WHEN

## TODAY I AM GRATEFUL FOR

## REFLECT AND CELEBRATE (EVENING)

## SCHEDULE

05:00 - MORNING ROUTINE

06:00

07:00

08:00

09:00

10:00

11:00

12:00

13:00

14:00

15:00

16:00

17:00

18:00

19:00

20:00 - EVENING ROUTINE

# DAILY SELF CALL SHEET

DATE

M  T  W  T  F  S  S

## TOP THREE PRIORITIES

1.

2.

3.

## TODAY'S INNER MONOLOGUE MESSAGE

## TODAY'S HIGHLIGHT AHEAD

## TODAY'S ONE WORD OBJECTIVE

## POTENTIAL OBSTACLE

## HOW I CAN PREPARE FOR THIS

## A DIRECTOR WOULD REMIND ME

## I COULD CALL TODAY A SUCCESSFUL WRAP WHEN

## TODAY I AM GRATEFUL FOR

## REFLECT AND CELEBRATE (EVENING)

## SCHEDULE

05:00 - MORNING ROUTINE

06:00

07:00

08:00

09:00

10:00

11:00

12:00

13:00

14:00

15:00

16:00

17:00

18:00

19:00

20:00 - EVENING ROUTINE

# DAILY SELF CALL SHEET

**TOP THREE PRIORITIES**

1.

2.

3.

**TODAY'S INNER MONOLOGUE MESSAGE**

**TODAY'S HIGHLIGHT AHEAD**

**TODAY'S ONE WORD OBJECTIVE**

**POTENTIAL OBSTACLE**

**HOW I CAN PREPARE FOR THIS**

**A DIRECTOR WOULD REMIND ME**

**I COULD CALL TODAY A SUCCESSFUL WRAP WHEN**

**TODAY I AM GRATEFUL FOR**

**REFLECT AND CELEBRATE (EVENING)**

**SCHEDULE**

05:00 - MORNING ROUTINE

06:00

07:00

08:00

09:00

10:00

11:00

12:00

13:00

14:00

15:00

16:00

17:00

18:00

19:00

20:00 - EVENING ROUTINE

# DAILY SELF CALL SHEET

DATE

M  T  W  T  F  S  S

## TOP THREE PRIORITIES

1.

2.

3.

## TODAY'S INNER MONOLOGUE MESSAGE

## TODAY'S HIGHLIGHT AHEAD

## TODAY'S ONE WORD OBJECTIVE

## POTENTIAL OBSTACLE

## HOW I CAN PREPARE FOR THIS

## A DIRECTOR WOULD REMIND ME

## I COULD CALL TODAY A SUCCESSFUL WRAP WHEN

## TODAY I AM GRATEFUL FOR

## REFLECT AND CELEBRATE (EVENING)

## SCHEDULE

05:00 - MORNING ROUTINE

06:00

07:00

08:00

09:00

10:00

11:00

12:00

13:00

14:00

15:00

16:00

17:00

18:00

19:00

20:00 - EVENING ROUTINE

# DAILY SELF CALL SHEET

## TOP THREE PRIORITIES

1.

2.

3.

## TODAY'S INNER MONOLOGUE MESSAGE

## TODAY'S HIGHLIGHT AHEAD

## TODAY'S ONE WORD OBJECTIVE

## POTENTIAL OBSTACLE

## HOW I CAN PREPARE FOR THIS

## A DIRECTOR WOULD REMIND ME

## I COULD CALL TODAY A SUCCESSFUL WRAP WHEN

## TODAY I AM GRATEFUL FOR

## REFLECT AND CELEBRATE (EVENING)

## SCHEDULE

05:00 - MORNING ROUTINE

06:00

07:00

08:00

09:00

10:00

11:00

12:00

13:00

14:00

15:00

16:00

17:00

18:00

19:00

20:00 - EVENING ROUTINE

# DAILY SELF CALL SHEET

DATE

M   T   W   T   F   S   S

## TOP THREE PRIORITIES

1.

2.

3.

## TODAY'S INNER MONOLOGUE MESSAGE

## TODAY'S HIGHLIGHT AHEAD

## TODAY'S ONE WORD OBJECTIVE

## POTENTIAL OBSTACLE

## HOW I CAN PREPARE FOR THIS

## A DIRECTOR WOULD REMIND ME

## I COULD CALL TODAY A SUCCESSFUL WRAP WHEN

## TODAY I AM GRATEFUL FOR

## REFLECT AND CELEBRATE (EVENING)

## SCHEDULE

05:00 - MORNING ROUTINE

06:00

07:00

08:00

09:00

10:00

11:00

12:00

13:00

14:00

15:00

16:00

17:00

18:00

19:00

20:00 - EVENING ROUTINE

# DAILY SELF CALL SHEET

DATE

M  T  W  T  F  S  S

## TOP THREE PRIORITIES

1.

2.

3.

## TODAY'S INNER MONOLOGUE MESSAGE

## TODAY'S HIGHLIGHT AHEAD

## TODAY'S ONE WORD OBJECTIVE

## POTENTIAL OBSTACLE

## HOW I CAN PREPARE FOR THIS

## A DIRECTOR WOULD REMIND ME

## I COULD CALL TODAY A SUCCESSFUL WRAP WHEN

## TODAY I AM GRATEFUL FOR

## REFLECT AND CELEBRATE (EVENING)

## SCHEDULE

05:00 - MORNING ROUTINE

06:00

07:00

08:00

09:00

10:00

11:00

12:00

13:00

14:00

15:00

16:00

17:00

18:00

19:00

20:00 - EVENING ROUTINE

# DIRECTOR'S CUT

**TOP THREE WINS THIS WEEK**

1. _____

2. _____

3. _____

**WHAT DID I LEARN THIS WEEK**

**WHAT CAN I LET GO OF**

**WHAT WORKED WELL THIS WEEK**

**WHAT CAN I LOOK FORWARD TO**

**IS THERE ANYTHING I'M AVOIDING**

**HOW CAN I ACCOMPLISH THIS NEXT WEEK**

**WHAT'S MY BIGGEST PRIORITY THIS WEEK AHEAD**

**ADDITIONAL NOTES**

_____

_____

_____

_____

# DAILY SELF CALL SHEET

DATE

M   T   W   T   F   S   S

## TOP THREE PRIORITIES

1.

2.

3.

## TODAY'S INNER MONOLOGUE MESSAGE

## TODAY'S HIGHLIGHT AHEAD

## TODAY'S ONE WORD OBJECTIVE

## POTENTIAL OBSTACLE

## HOW I CAN PREPARE FOR THIS

## A DIRECTOR WOULD REMIND ME

## I COULD CALL TODAY A SUCCESSFUL WRAP WHEN

## TODAY I AM GRATEFUL FOR

## REFLECT AND CELEBRATE (EVENING)

## SCHEDULE

05:00 - MORNING ROUTINE

06:00

07:00

08:00

09:00

10:00

11:00

12:00

13:00

14:00

15:00

16:00

17:00

18:00

19:00

20:00 - EVENING ROUTINE

# DAILY SELF CALL SHEET

DATE

M   T   W   T   F   S   S

## TOP THREE PRIORITIES

1.

2.

3.

## TODAY'S INNER MONOLOGUE MESSAGE

## TODAY'S HIGHLIGHT AHEAD

## TODAY'S ONE WORD OBJECTIVE

## POTENTIAL OBSTACLE

## HOW I CAN PREPARE FOR THIS

## A DIRECTOR WOULD REMIND ME

## I COULD CALL TODAY A SUCCESSFUL WRAP WHEN

## TODAY I AM GRATEFUL FOR

## REFLECT AND CELEBRATE (EVENING)

## SCHEDULE

05:00 - MORNING ROUTINE

06:00

07:00

08:00

09:00

10:00

11:00

12:00

13:00

14:00

15:00

16:00

17:00

18:00

19:00

20:00 - EVENING ROUTINE

# DAILY SELF CALL SHEET

## TOP THREE PRIORITIES

1.

2.

3.

## TODAY'S INNER MONOLOGUE MESSAGE

## TODAY'S HIGHLIGHT AHEAD

## TODAY'S ONE WORD OBJECTIVE

## POTENTIAL OBSTACLE

## HOW I CAN PREPARE FOR THIS

## A DIRECTOR WOULD REMIND ME

## I COULD CALL TODAY A SUCCESSFUL WRAP WHEN

## TODAY I AM GRATEFUL FOR

## REFLECT AND CELEBRATE (EVENING)

## SCHEDULE

05:00 - MORNING ROUTINE

06:00

07:00

08:00

09:00

10:00

11:00

12:00

13:00

14:00

15:00

16:00

17:00

18:00

19:00

20:00 - EVENING ROUTINE

# DAILY SELF CALL SHEET

DATE

M   T   W   T   F   S   S

## TOP THREE PRIORITIES

1.
2.
3.

## TODAY'S INNER MONOLOGUE MESSAGE

## TODAY'S HIGHLIGHT AHEAD

## TODAY'S ONE WORD OBJECTIVE

## POTENTIAL OBSTACLE

## HOW I CAN PREPARE FOR THIS

## A DIRECTOR WOULD REMIND ME

## I COULD CALL TODAY A SUCCESSFUL WRAP WHEN

## TODAY I AM GRATEFUL FOR

## REFLECT AND CELEBRATE (EVENING)

## SCHEDULE

05:00 - MORNING ROUTINE

06:00

07:00

08:00

09:00

10:00

11:00

12:00

13:00

14:00

15:00

16:00

17:00

18:00

19:00

20:00 - EVENING ROUTINE

# DAILY SELF CALL SHEET

DATE _____

M  T  W  T  F  S  S

## TOP THREE PRIORITIES

1. _____

2. _____

3. _____

## TODAY'S INNER MONOLOGUE MESSAGE

## TODAY'S HIGHLIGHT AHEAD

## TODAY'S ONE WORD OBJECTIVE

## POTENTIAL OBSTACLE

## HOW I CAN PREPARE FOR THIS

## A DIRECTOR WOULD REMIND ME

## I COULD CALL TODAY A SUCCESSFUL WRAP WHEN

## TODAY I AM GRATEFUL FOR

## REFLECT AND CELEBRATE (EVENING)

## SCHEDULE

05:00 - MORNING ROUTINE

06:00

07:00

08:00

09:00

10:00

11:00

12:00

13:00

14:00

15:00

16:00

17:00

18:00

19:00

20:00 - EVENING ROUTINE

# DAILY SELF CALL SHEET

DATE

M  T  W  T  F  S  S

## TOP THREE PRIORITIES

1.

2.

3.

## TODAY'S INNER MONOLOGUE MESSAGE

## TODAY'S HIGHLIGHT AHEAD

## TODAY'S ONE WORD OBJECTIVE

## POTENTIAL OBSTACLE

## HOW I CAN PREPARE FOR THIS

## A DIRECTOR WOULD REMIND ME

## I COULD CALL TODAY A SUCCESSFUL WRAP WHEN

## TODAY I AM GRATEFUL FOR

## REFLECT AND CELEBRATE (EVENING)

## SCHEDULE

05:00 - MORNING ROUTINE

06:00

07:00

08:00

09:00

10:00

11:00

12:00

13:00

14:00

15:00

16:00

17:00

18:00

19:00

20:00 - EVENING ROUTINE

# DAILY SELF CALL SHEET

DATE

M T W T F S S

## TOP THREE PRIORITIES

1.

2.

3.

## TODAY'S INNER MONOLOGUE MESSAGE

## TODAY'S HIGHLIGHT AHEAD

## TODAY'S ONE WORD OBJECTIVE

## POTENTIAL OBSTACLE

## HOW I CAN PREPARE FOR THIS

## A DIRECTOR WOULD REMIND ME

## I COULD CALL TODAY A SUCCESSFUL WRAP WHEN

## TODAY I AM GRATEFUL FOR

## REFLECT AND CELEBRATE (EVENING)

## SCHEDULE

05:00 - MORNING ROUTINE

06:00

07:00

08:00

09:00

10:00

11:00

12:00

13:00

14:00

15:00

16:00

17:00

18:00

19:00

20:00 - EVENING ROUTINE

# DIRECTOR'S CUT

**TOP THREE WINS THIS WEEK**

1. _____

2. _____

3. _____

**WHAT DID I LEARN THIS WEEK**

**WHAT CAN I LET GO OF**

**WHAT WORKED WELL THIS WEEK**

**WHAT CAN I LOOK FORWARD TO**

**IS THERE ANYTHING I'M AVOIDING**

**HOW CAN I ACCOMPLISH THIS NEXT WEEK**

**WHAT'S MY BIGGEST PRIORITY THIS WEEK AHEAD**

**ADDITIONAL NOTES**

_____

_____

_____

# JOURNAL PAGES

# JOURNAL PAGES

# JOURNAL PAGES

# JOURNAL PAGES

# JOURNAL PAGES

You Are The Creator — the Writer, Producer, Director and Actor of your own story. BE THE LEAD, be the Hero and Create Consciously.

BETHELEAD.CLUB